JOHN BALABAN

Path,
Crooked Path

 Copper Canyon Press

The author gratefully acknowledges the use of lyrics from the song "Hurt," by Trent Reznor. Originally published by Nine Inch Nails on *Downward Spiral*, TVT/Interscope Records, Inc. (ASCAP), 92346-2. © 1994.

Cover art: *Untitled*, photograph by Maya Goded. Chihuahua, Mexico — Los Zorros/MAGNUM. © 2004.

Grateful acknowledgment is made to photographer Carola Clift.

Copper Canyon Press is in residence at Fort Worden State Park in Port Townsend, Washington, under the auspices of Centrum Foundation. Centrum is a gathering place for artists and creative thinkers from around the world, students of all ages and backgrounds, and audiences seeking extraordinary cultural enrichment.

LIBRARY OF CONGRESS CATALOGING-IN-PUBLICATION DATA

Balaban, John, 1943–

Path, crooked path / by John Balaban.

   p. cm.

Includes bibliographical references.

ISBN 1-55659-238-8 (alk. paper)

1. Title.

PS3552.A44P38   2006

811'.54—dc22

                                                  2005024579

98765432 FIRST PRINTING

COPPER CANYON PRESS

Post Office Box 271

Port Townsend, Washington 98368

www.coppercanyonpress.org

811
Balaban

Path, Crooked Path

Other Books by John Balaban

POETRY

After Our War (University of Pittsburgh Press, 1974)

Blue Mountain (Unicorn Press, 1982)

Words for My Daughter (Copper Canyon Press, 1991)

Locusts at the Edge of Summer: New & Selected Poems
(Copper Canyon Press, 1997, 2003)

TRANSLATION

Vietnam: A Traveler's Literary Companion, with Nguyen Qui Duc
(Whereabouts Press, 1996)

Spring Essence: The Poetry of Hồ Xuân Hương (Copper Canyon Press, 2000)

Ca Dao Việt Nam: Vietnamese Folk Poetry (Copper Canyon Press, 2003)

NONFICTION

Vietnam: The Land We Never Knew (Chronicle Books, 1989)

Remembering Heaven's Face: A Story of Rescue in Wartime Vietnam
(University of Georgia Press, 2002)

FICTION

The Hawk's Tale (Harcourt Brace Jovanovich, 1988)

Coming Down Again (Simon & Schuster/Fireside, 1989)

As if I were standing here in my own yard
Holding in my open hands this blessing of my journey,
A dry little foam of where I come from,
Where I am today, and where I am headed in the snow.

ROLAND FLINT, "Varna Snow"

The author wishes to thank the Lannan Foundation
and the John Simon Guggenheim Memorial Foundation
for their support.

ACKNOWLEDGMENTS

Some of these poems have appeared in *Alaska Quarterly Review, The Atlantic Monthly, Fugue, Gargoyle Magazine, Green Mountains Review, Leviathan, The Massachusetts Review, Michigan Quarterly Review, New Letters, The New York Review of Books, Poetry Flash, Poets of Bulgaria* (Unicorn Press, 1986), *The Raleigh News & Observer, The Ruminator Review, Solo, TriQuarterly, The Virginia Quarterly Review,* and *Witness.* A version of "Looking Out from the Acropolis, 1989" appeared previously in *Locusts at the Edge of Summer.*

Contents

Miami Suite

⌄ ⌄ ⌄

Path, Crooked Path

They asked the traveler where he came from,

where he was going. He replied, "I am coming from

behind my back, going in the direction I am facing."

The Hundred Thousand Songs of Milarepa

Highway 61 Revisited

Summer was flooding the city highways
bathing sycamores below the savage tenements,
leafage flushed green, almost obscuring
the plastic grocery bags snagged in branch-tops
flapping in the roadside wind, in the whine
of semis and buses and cars and vans
plastic shreds fluttering, prayer flags of the poor,
as rackety apartment ACs hummed an *AUM* chorus
in the June cement heat, and I sped by, heading out
once more for the heart of the heart of the country,
rolling down Highway 61, heading West and South,
lighting out again, away from fanfare and drumbeats,
the couples holding hands in their slow-motion leaps
from the skyscraper windows billowing smoke.

In midwestern farmlands rustling wheatcrowns,
spreading out with alfalfa and sorghum, sprouting corn,
I thought I was lost, in the crickets and songbirds,
but tire whine and bumper glare kept me on course
and when I picked up the soldier mugged in the bus station,
teeth kicked in, wallet taken, hitching back to base in Waco
to his tank-repair unit readying for another Iraq war
I knew I was on the right road, running like a lifeline
across the palm of America.

                    In Texas, I heard voices.
In the dead-ugly creosote basin of Midland–Odessa
where — all across the hot mesquite horizon — oil jockeys
pumped crude from the sandy wastes, and a billboard

boasted "Home of President and Mrs. George W. Bush."
I had a powerful urge to pee and pulled off the highway.
Taking my whiz at an Exxon, then gassing up again,
I looked around when I heard a voice calling, "Help me."
Calling softly, "Can you help me?" I looked around
and saw an elderly man in a battered Honda, door open,
big shoes planted on the greasy cement, looking at me.
"What do you need?" I asked, thinking maybe a few bucks,
but he wanted me to *lift his legs* into his little car.
Prosthetic legs, I could feel, heavy as cinder blocks.
"Where you headed?" I asked as he turned the key,
but he just pointed his finger like a gun, said,
"*That* way, down Highway 61."

I turned onto a less traveled blacktop running south
past volcanic peaks to Mexico and the Big Bend.
From my windshield to the horizon, dust devils
swirled over the greasewood and yucca spikes,
whipping up little tornadoes of dust and grit
around the odd horse or pronghorns grazing with cattle
behind hundreds of miles of barbed-wire fences — a dry land,
old haunt of raiding Apaches, Comanches, Pancho Villa.

But tonight is the summer solstice and I am with friends
in this high-desert border town rumbled by freight trains.
Outside the moon has risen over the Sierra Madres,
shining on burros shuffling through willows, below cottonwoods
along the Rio Grande, glistening on the backs of thumb-size
toads in the stone pans where water seeps in the canyons,
shining on the humble folk wading into Texas,
shining on the Border Patrols, on the DEA blimp,
shining on the bright empty ribbon of Highway 61,
loud with strange cries echoing across America.

Looking Out from the Acropolis, 1989

> Each structure, in its beauty, was even then and at
> once antique, but in the freshness of its vigor, even
> today, recent and newly wrought.
>
> PLUTARCH, ON THE ACROPOLIS

In old-town Athens of date palms, of ferned balconies
cascading canary calls, I walked with a Bulgarian friend
up the stony, sunny path to the "high city" where tangles
of cactus and Spanish sword pocked the Periclean ramparts
and packs of wild cats prowled the brush for mice as wind
whipped the naps of their fur and Georgi's little son, Aleko,
hooted after them as we trailed behind, plodding upward
through the gate of broken columns to the precincts of Athena,
two poets, from West and East, here for the first time, awed
by the lonely grace of stones fallen, stones still standing.

⌄

On the left, the smiling maidens of the caryatid porch
whose marble robes fluttered in blue sky;
on the right, the massive surge of Parthenon columns
capped by a parade of centaurs, horsemen, gods,
reliving dramas of who we are, who we might become
as pediments marked our battles with beasts, our talks
with gods, our search for ourselves in philosopher groves
of this city on the hill that draws us by surviving
Persian navies, Roman consuls, pasha's yoke, *Panzergruppe*
—holding up like a Phidean model a sense
of the examined life that is worth living, a place
where gods and men can struggle with success, striving

to widen the wealth of the human soul, the size of heaven.
All across the monumental rubble, trailing after tour guides,
Japanese photographed this field of broken stone.

⌄

As we looked out from the Acropolis, we saw
the New World Order the President praised
that winter as caged canaries down below
sang in the sunshine of Athenian balconies:
Both superpowers, bankrupt; the Japanese, our bankers.
Looking east past Yugoslavian slaughter,
the Kozlodui reactor was about to blow.
Further east, in Tbilisi, the shoot-out at Parliament,
the breadlines in Moscow, the dead rivers and lakes,
the black colonels hopping in Rumpelstilskin rage
at loss of empire, as Chechens, Kurds, Azeris et al.
went for their guns to settle old scores.
How much has changed since then?
Merely the killing fields.

⌄

Then it was Israeli rubber bullets and intifada stones.
Holiday shoppers at Clapham Junction bombed by Irish Santas.
German skinheads bashing Vietnamese and Turks.
Bloated African bellies, fly-infested eyes.
Shining Path Maoists beheading Indians in Ayacucho.
And nosferatu warlords in Beijing sipping their elixir
of cinnabar and blood. Pol Pot vacationing in Thailand.

⌄

Meanwhile, it was snowing in Chicago, snowing on the cardboard huts
of the homeless in the land of the free, as more banks failed
and repossessed midwestern farms lay fallow to the wind.
Each in the cell of himself was almost convinced of his freedom
when the Wall fell to cheers of freed multitudes
and one could hear communist and capitalist gasps rise up
in a global shout that circled the earth for a year
then disappeared through holes in the ozone layer.

⌄

The New World Order. The tribes of the Book
are still turned to wrath as the worst of us
would wind time back to savage pasts easier to imagine.
The philosopher's grove is empty; the poet's words gone flat.
Against this, aren't the Japanese, baptized in nuclear fire,
clapping their hands for the Kami of the cash register,
our safest, sanest neighbors?

⌄

These old stones cry out for more.
Surviving centuries, sculpted for all to see,
declaring our need for beauty and laws like love
for this tiny *polis* of a planet spinning wildly,
for my daughter, snug, asleep in her bed,
for Aleko who played in the Chernobyl cloud,
whose father stood near Nike's rotting frieze,
looking out upon the city jammed with cars. Georgi
opened his flask of vodka and poured some on a stone
before we drank our toasts to the new world order
and to whatever muse might come to give us words.

Georgi Borrisov in Paris

The Slavic poet sips his morning vodka, his mind
as troubled as the river sliding down below
the 22nd floor of his apartment on the Seine
where a barge cuts the surface to thread Pont Mirabeau.

He knows that words are fading from books.
From poems of Pushkin, from Apollonaire's,
from poems he wrote when talking in his dreams.
Words are disappearing, leaving pages bare.

Next door, an office complex bustles like a hive,
its workers tending cells inside the glassed-in combs.
He stares into their cubicles. It sours his vodka.
Their tower has become… a heap of drying bones.

But what can poets do about the missing words, gone
even from those lips that longed to say them — like wishes
floating off above the river, like coins
tossed from barges, bridges, *bateaux mouches?*

Where else is this happening? Is it happening at home?
In a world reduced to billboards, he would be totally unnerved.
The strangely exiled poet has been drinking for ten days
but this has only sharpened his worry about the words…

Some Dogs of the World

VENICE BEACH, CALIFORNIA

Out there, waves wobble up and crash in sunglare.
And here: rows of tattoo parlors, sunglass stands,
tanned babes and oiled boys sweeping by on Rollerblades,
past tourists, palm readers, ice-cream parlors, the air alive
with Carlos Santana whose "Black Magic Woman"
is wiggling her middle-aged butt through a loudspeaker
as two leathery blondes sashay out from the '60s
— one with daisies pinned to her beret, the other with ribbons
fluttering from her graying hair and a smile pinned on
for the sunstruck shuffle of T-shirted tourists in shorts
pausing now to gawk at a high-heeled *donna alla moda*
walking her Chihuahua like a rat on a rope.

CLUJ, TRANSYLVANIA, ROMANIA

Outside the Panegrano Patiserie
a man with greasy jacket and beret
feeds two strays some bits of sweet roll.
One mutt chews the bread thoughtfully.
This isn't what she was looking for, but it's food,
and the nice, smelly man is laughing.
Then her mate takes off howling
after a third dog trotting down the street,
chasing the interloper helter-skelter
through legs of passersby, barking
and yammering, bowling over some guy
like a set of tenpins. The whole street's shouting
in Magyar and Romanian. And the dogs scatter.
Later, on the road to Bucharest, a bay horse

lies dead in the roadside gravel
where a Gypsy cart got smashed by a car,
a wild dog yanking at its tail and hocks.

LUNCH WITH A DISTRICT CHIEF, OUTSIDE HANOI

My American friend, who is vegetarian but making concessions,
thinks the translator said, "Can you eat dark meat?"
But, of course, it is "dog," not *dark*. Puppy, not *poulet*.
By the third or fourth bite, the translation is corrected,
and my friend swallows, smiles, and says it's good
out of deference to our host, a decent man
who was shot through the lungs during our war,
who was sent home to die, and who now is smiling
at the chance, at last, to talk to these Americans.

PARIS, LE PETIT ZINC RESTAURANT

Fancy people. Fancy food.
And here comes Spot bopping along
la rue Buci, a veritable boulevardier
pausing to lift a hind leg and pee, while cocking
one admiring eye on the elegant sidewalk diners.
Ah, *mes semblables*.

On the Death of His Dog, Apples

> Nae mair I'll wander through the glen,
> Nor disturb the roost o' the pheasant hen.
>
> "MY LAST FAREWELL TO STIRLING"

Old mutt, asleep on your rug
but game into dotage
you'd sometimes yelp and work your legs
running rabbits in dreamland.

Thinned to bone by a bellyful of cancer,
when the vet syringed your shaved vein
you looked at me as if we'd flushed a grouse,
ears perked, eyes startled.

And when your eyes fogged
and your muzzle slumped in the crook of my arm,
I dreamed for you an upland meadow,
a clear brook of bright water,

hillsides full of pheasants
where rabbits frisked in bluebells,
where you dozed then rose to greet me,
wagging your tail as I crossed the creek.

The Lives of the Poets

> The country is proud of its dead poets. It takes
> terrific satisfaction in the poets' testimony that the
> USA is too tough, too big, too much, too rugged, that
> American reality is overpowering… So poets are
> loved, but loved because they just can't make it here.
>
> SAUL BELLOW, *Humboldt's Gift**

Fact is, it's a reality that grinds us all,
even those who whisper to themselves: *If* I
were not such a corrupt, unfeeling bastard, creep,
thief, and vulture, I couldn't get through this either.
Still they collapse at meetings, on tennis courts,
pig valves going ka-boom in their hearts,
pitching into their *Wall Street Journal*s
as the train lurches home to the Hamptons,
as the cab crawls uptown to the condo on the Park.
Dying in their dandruff, on their treadmills,
taking their sips of dioxin seepage,
eyes fried by computer screens and boredom.
The huge need for cocaine said it all.

⌄

Well, these were the thoughts that came to me
on a high wooded bluff outside Port Townsend
just after Levertov died. Her *Times* obit
ran next to some admiral's from the Vietnam War,
apparent adversaries, now side by side,

---

*All italicized quotes are from Saul Bellow, *Humboldt's Gift* (Viking, 1975),
p. 117.

true to their conflicting truths.
The hand that gives. The hand that takes.

All about me clumps of sweet pea, purples
and pinks, cascaded down the grassy hillsides
as dawn mist raveled a wreath through inky tops
of Douglas firs. Far off, the distant Strait
of Juan de Fuca pulled tides below a cloudbank
and ferry foghorns called, each to each.
Can sung words calm the guns of a steeled fleet?
(*Orpheus moved stones and trees. But a poet
can't perform a hysterectomy or send a vehicle
out of the solar system.*) At Sotheby's,
Ginsberg's top hat went for $258 after
the bad gray poet launched his last exhalation.

⌄

Unsettled, I drove to Seattle's Blue Moon Tavern
where soon I annoyed a man in straggly hair
and baseball cap, reading Cicero through wire-rims,
hunched at the beat-up bar and railing at me,
"Man, I *told* you. I don't *know* those people!"
My mistake. He looked like he might have
perched on that barstool reading Latin
for decades since abandoning a dissertation.
But he didn't know Roethke, or Hugo, or Wright,
whose framed lugubrious black-and-whites
still hung from the rough plank walls
where once they drank and howled like Humboldt.
The only woman among them: Carolyn Kizer,
with her huge sultry eyes and severe French hat,
Dorothy Parker to this Algonquin of moonstruck boozers.

⌄

The weakness of the spiritual powers is proved
in the childishness, madness, drunkenness, and despair
of these martyrs… They succumbed, poor loonies.
One thinks of Roethke weeping over a dead mouse
cupped in his huge hands. Of Hugo sweating out
a hangover in the bleachers of a sandlot game.
Lew Welch walking off forever into the scorpion Sierras.
Hart Crane over the side of a ship. And Jarrell
falling in front of a car. And poor John Berryman
jumping from a bridge. (And Plath and Sexton
gassing themselves.) Delmore Schwartz,
Humboldt Humbert, shouting from the moon.

⌄

So, praise to those still coming through on song,
a bigger tribe than one can name and tough
as anything put up by corporate America:
Maxine Kumin with her horse-broke neck, still
writing, still hitching up and riding Deuter.
William Meredith struggling back toward speech.
Hayden Carruth raising a toast with his "poet's
cheap, sufficient chardonnay." Richard Wilbur
calling us to morning air awash with angels.
Merwin in Hawaii, Snyder in the Sierras,
both taking the nothingness of *sunyata*
to conjure up a habitation.

       Walking
their Sonoma farm with Kizer's husband John,
we stopped before a storm-struck, twisted pear tree,

a remnant from an orchard of 100 years ago.
Out of the hulk of its blackened trunk,
one smooth-skinned branch sent forth some leaves.
"Still blooming?" I asked. "Madly," he said.

Romania, Romania

Looking at a map of Romania, one finds below Bîrlad, lost in the remote rolling hills near the crooked path of the Danube, not far from its Black Sea delta, the town of Bălăbănești, the "Place of the Balabans," chartered by Stefan the Great in 1520 after one of my ancestors rallied a peasant force that defeated "The Turk." Bălăbănești is a small farming town, just down the dusty road from the hamlet of Bălăbănye, both folded into the fields and hedgerows, along quiet streams forded by medieval, high-arched Turkish bridges.

Since the beginning of time, armies and marauders have swept through these fertile farmlands at the edge of Europe. Scythians, Thracians, Sarmatians. Names we hardly recognize. Empires, vanished overnight.

In A.D. 8, having annoyed Caesar Augustus, Ovid was banished to the Black Sea port of Tomis, now the Romanian city of Constanța. Ovid's *Tristia* and *Epistulae ex Ponto* are his last poems. Poems of an exile, aged, miserably separated from his family and following, relegated to a corner of the Pax Romana where Latin was not spoken, where literature was unknown. In his last works, he says he composed a poem in Getic, the local language. He says this with some embarrassment. Also, that one winter he stepped out with trepidation on the frozen Black Sea, and that he joined the citizenry at the ramparts to defend Tomis against barbarian horsemen who besieged the city with poison darts.

Hoc ubi vivendum est satis est si consequor arvo... esse poeta. "Here, where I have to live, it will be enough to remain a poet."

Ovid, *Tristia* V.x:15-22

Countless tribes roam about threatening savage war.
They think it disgraceful to live without plundering.
Outside, it's never safe. Our citadel defends itself
from weak ramparts, though strategically placed.
When the host descends, unexpected like birds,
we barely see them before they've seized their prey.
Often, gates shut, safe inside the walls,
we gather arrows fallen in the streets.

Innumerae circa gentes fera bella minantur,
    quae sibi non rapto vivere turpe putant.
Nil extra tutum est: tumulus defenditur ipse
    moenibus exiguis ingenioque loci.
Cum minime credas, ut aves, densissimus hostis
    advolat, et praedam vix bene visus agit.
Saepe intra muros clausis venientia portis
    per medias legimus noxia tela vias.

The Siege

from the Romanian of Stefan Augustin Doinas

But when they went out of the city to surrender they
found the enemy nowhere to be seen.
POLYBIUS

The city at spear point. The army unseen.
Wells stopped, and smoke rising.
Our eagle standard, alive but not with valor,
we ate, without it sticking in our throats.
Then, the plagues. Ghosts from times past,
more faithful to their hearths than we, shot
arrows from ramparts, from far across the fields.
Nothing. Only a star-wound in a god's flesh.
Later, the clock of betrayal struck. Our drawbridge
fell from its pulleys. Cowards, faces to the earth,
begged forgiveness. But no one heard, only the moon
crossing the moat like the bow of a ship on the wind.
Yes, no one. Until the last of our deaths
we shall weep blood and suffer strangely,
doors open to evils, windows shattered.
Not a soul outside the city. But we, we surrendered.

Ibn Fadhlan, the Arab Emissary, Encounters Vikings on the Volga River, A.D. 922

The Rus, as they are called, camped above the river
trading furs from a log hall, axed out by slaves.
The men — tall as date palms, blond, tattooed —
had set a pole out front carved with gods
to which they offer things to bless their trade.
This was all I saw of their piety or conscience.
Caliph, they are the dirtiest creatures of God.

Each morning when the men stir out of sleep
a slave girl brings a bronze ablution bowl
first to the chief who washes his face, then
rinses his mouth, spits, and blows his nose
into the bowl which she carries around until
each has washed in the same filthy water.

When their lord died, a huge *sahirra dakhma*
(the witch who rules the slave girls) set them wailing
as they packed his corpse in black earth and
his men built a death ship with a funeral pyre.
They call this witch "Angel of Death," *Malak al-Mawt*.
She picked a girl to go with the dead lord, then
invited the men to fornicate with the slave girl
drugged and lost in a crazy song.

Then the girl was led to the ship
where the lord, his corpse now washed,
lay on the pyre wreathed in flowers and fruit.
Then the woman stabbed the girl

in her ribs as a man crept behind her
with a knotted rope, strangling her cries
until she fell dead and they laid her on the pyre.

Torching the ship, knocking away its blocks,
they shoved it blazing in the river, singing
their lord to a life of pleasures they imagine.
Soon his ship was ashes swirling on the currents.
O Caliph, through forested lands, west and north,
one finds only infidels with vile habits.
Some are Christian. Nothing will come of them.

Loving Graham Greene

for Gloria Emerson

> But in Indochina I drained a magic potion, a loving
> cup which I have shared since with many retired
> *colons* and officers of the Foreign Legion whose eyes
> light up at the mention of Saigon and Hanoi.
>
> GRAHAM GREENE, INTRODUCTION,
> *The Quiet American*

So there he was, decades after the war,
rattled and adrift, waiting in the waiting room
of a shrink in New Mexico, of all places,

an office in a garden by an adobe house
its tin roof aflame with sunlight
as the sun humped across blue sky

and hummingbirds raced to plunder heads
of purple cosmos and bee balm while sunflowers
looked up like a congregation seeking benediction.

Beyond the garden, the river surged over
canyon rocks and piñon snags where big trout
lurked in the cold shadows of dark pools.

He was on vacation; he hadn't planned this visit.
The wife and kids were taking the trail ride.
He had found the name in the phone book.

After a lot of babble and blubbering, the guy
asked him if he knew what was wrong,
what was hurting him so, why he was crying,

why he was here. He shook
his head "no." No,
he didn't know.

"Still a reporter?" *Yes.*
"Successful?" *Yes, pretty much.*
"Happily married?" *Well, yeah.*

"But your eyes," he said, "are dead,
except when you mention Vietnam,
and then a little spurt of epinephrine

zings your system and your eyes light up."
The therapist charged sixty bucks,
suggested he take up skydiving.

Driving back to the riddled heap of villagers
from which someone had pulled out a live 3-year-old,
past the berm wire where they were still yanking off

the bodies, he was flying in a chopper when it dove down
to open up on a lone elephant in a field of sugarcane.
After a gin fizz on the veranda of the Continental Palace,

he was back at the motel where everyone was by the pool,
the kids all lit up after their trail ride high on the canyon rim,
where the air was sweet with pine and bear grass, the sky clear.

A Vision

translated, with Elena Christova, from the Bulgarian
of Kolyo Sevov

Sea spray glistens the marble god.
Waves surge through his feet.
Salt mists trace his stern visage.
Fog laves the statue until it darkens.

Marble gods darken with time.

At night, when waves roll with seaweed
and jellyfish open white umbrellas as
periwinkles poke from their shells, it is quiet.
So quiet one hears the footfalls of the dead.

Tonight, a sailor lies beached upon the sand.

Tides have rocked him all his life.
His hopes have turned to salt.
The sea has stolen all from him.
Waves lick his heels.

Naked. He is nothing.

A god. A tangle of seaweed.
A corpse washed up.
The night crashes with madness.
The day was reefed on hopes.

Soldier Home

> At first Krebs… did not want to talk about the war at
> all. Later he felt the need to talk but no one wanted to
> hear about it.
>
> ERNEST HEMINGWAY, "SOLDIER'S HOME"

Full moon over Beaufort Inlet, moon path streaming toward him
barefoot on the cold beach, watching wave crests rush the shore.

Out in the Atlantic silence, boat lights wink on a black horizon
as a Camp Lejeune chopper circles and circles a spot on the sea,

engine staccato louder than the waves, searchlights
brighter than the moon. Finally it breaks off, heads landward,

a wasp shape bisecting the moon, lights cut at the shoreline,
engine loud in the boy's head. Not even the waves can drown it.

"Captains and soldiers are smeared on the bushes and grass;
Our generals schemed in vain," Li Po wrote, twelve centuries ago.

Let Him Be

translated, with Alexandra Veleva, from the
Bulgarian of Georgi Borrisov

Let the man be who had nothing to tell you,
let him mumble his beard over his mug of gall,
let him work his bread into bits at the table.
Let him think he's coughing because the tobacco's damp.

And let him, as he leaves, nod goodbye to the bottle
and go outside and leap from the porch into the night
and stride across the fields already thick with clover
to wave down the first truck that finds him in its lights.

Let him tell the wicked driver all about his ulcer,
how it keeps him up, hungry at odd times,
and how bread is not enough, no, not by bread alone
despite whatever may be the common thought.

Let him get off at a hill and go up to a pear tree
and punch his fist right through the twisted trunk,
clean through to the night, and, as the tree listens,
let him curse it in pain and shame and bitter hurt.

Because, life picks us up like little chunks of ryebread
and wads and works us in its rough, sweaty fist.
So let him be, this man who's walking down the hillside.
Let him alone. Let him slam the table with his fist.

Waiting in a Desert Canyon

Waiting in canyon willows,
in a dry ravine, by a thin stream
that once he might have conjured up
but now has found by chance,

for words like creekwater
to spill bright spokes
through rocks and snags
into pools where voices gather.

Waiting for words to echo up
because he had been a fool
though once he was Saint Ives,
raven talking on his shoulder.

Waiting for words, summoning
voices he thought he knew were there,
asking: forgiveness for all the times
they called and he turned away.

Oh, when the bird flew off
he was the merest scarecrow,
a stumble of sticks now hunched
in a dusty canyon, waiting.

Poor Sap

for A.J. Lawrence, 1958–1985

He would rather have held her
than the gun in his hand
but she was gone. The gun was second best.
A way of being with her,
the slugs snug in their beveled chambers.
A real comfort, to have it handy.

He wanted to do it in the woods
under wavering treetops
shaking light through leaves.
Put the gun to his head…
in deep woods generous
with creek-and-birdsong
where he was never a reproach
but companion.
Then, he thought, hell,
blow your brains outside her office.
Make your point.

Fuck the gun, he finally said,
for with his thumb on the syringe
he found a way to find her
in throwaway hypos he filched from a nurse.
Could find her, say, strolling a beach,
brine on her lips, wet hair tangled down
to the long curve at the small of her back.
From dunes they'd watch gulls teeter
on updrafts above the waves, drifting.

Sotol

Miles of barbed wire strung to the horizon
fencing cattle and their graze of greasewood
puckered with yellow blossoms, scattered
with dry grasses, cat's claw, thistle, spurge,
fan-strands of spiny ocotillo, mescal, mesquite,
fishhook and prickly pear cactus, acacia, yucca
and sotol spikes spraying white blossoms.

Along a fence line: a passel of turkey vultures
perch, wings spread, taking the sun into
their black capes, these mask-of-red-death
horrors, their faces wattled in bluish warts, waiting
for the dead — pronghorn or jackrabbit, luck
run out, or maybe a boy from across the border.

Yet on this early morning yellow warblers
trill the desert willows along the arroyo.
Even the cottonwoods are taking off in song,
trembling great leafy tambourines in the cool air
while down by the Rio, a Border Patrol SUV
is dragging a sledge of old tires through a dry wash,
sweeping footprints for a day of tracking aliens.

Mexicans make a drink from sotol,
something like tequila or pulque from maguey,
an elixir of agave, a tincture of spike and thorn,
distilled from sun and wheeling shadows,
with a pinch of cactus bloom, a scent of sage.

A strong, perplexing drink: Birdsong
at the first sip. Thorn in the tongue, at the last.
And yet we drink. And drink again.

Root Boy Slim

1945–1993

Dead now, Foster MacKenzie III, better known as Root Boy Slim,
lead singer and composeur for his Sex Change Band.

His trademarks "Liquor Store Hold-Up in Space," "Dating the Undead,"
and the ever-popular "Boogie 'Til You Puke" rocked
the '80s bar scene in D.C., his coked and uninsultable clientele.

The *sight* of him invited trouble. Even his obituary misbehaved, noting
he "dressed like a slob and took delight in shocking his audiences."

I kept the clipping for a week, then tossed it in the basket
but plucked it out, alive in my hand like some stunned sparrow,
some stoned songbird tumbled down a long, long chimney.

If Only

Their cottage sat on a grassy bluff
weathered by salt spray, fogs, and rain
blowing off dunes and bleached logpiles
past tidal creeks seeping out to sea.

Cattails bobbed with redwing blackbirds.
Sparrows clamored through wild-rose thickets.
Two dogs, spattered with sandy muck,
snoozed on the sunny porch steps.

Dinner simmered on the stove.
Pulling weeds in the garden, she smiled,
hearing his tires pop gravel and clamshells
at their rutted lane's long winding end.

The dogs leapt up, loped out to greet him.
This is how it should have been.

Leaving

All her hopes
    were in the house
she was walking out of
    shutting the screen door
as the kitchen flared
    in smoke
of shouts and kisses,
    laughter, cooking, cleaning,
and, then, just
    the old, exhausting quarrels,
the wrangling, the accusations —
    while, inside,
the addled man sat on a stool,
    dying for a drink,
flames on his glasses,
    plucking his amplified guitar
as the windows flashed
    conflagrations
                    of lost wishes.

Out by the curb
    in the backseat
packed with clothes and books
    her goofy Setter
looked bewildered;
    her sad Lab
hung his chin out the window.

Behind their curtains
    neighbors watched
having said the proper things;
    the little girl
she sometimes minded
    was still crying
as her mother encouraged her
    to wave goodbye.

All along the shady street
    maple seeds let loose
and spun to the ground.
    All her hopes
had been in that house
    that she was driving away from,
maple seeds fluttering down,
    guitar fading,
    the road to Somewhere
    opening ahead.

Head-to-Toe

LEFT FOOT: three bones snapped, age 10,
sliding in to home plate. Scored, *but*

if you cannonball a kid off home plate
you must consider the consequences.

ABDOMEN, left side: a starfish scar from
an arrow shot in his belly, age 12.

That evening, his dad got home, heard the news,
then barreled off into the neighbor's house whacking
the kid and his father with the broken shaft.

Agog, woozy with the tetanus shot, the boy
watches the beatings, learning more about
consequences... (love? justice?).

HEAD: concussion, age 14. His buddies tossed him in
the local pool but his head didn't clear the apron.
A simple lesson in gravity and misplaced trust.

RIGHT LEG: age 16. Shinbone gouged from the kick pedal
of the little Harley he rode to school until crashing.

But he is growing up. (Keeping mum about his
near beheading from the clothesline wire, he says
he gave the bike to a friend, pleasing his mom.)

LEFT SHOULDER, 23: a red scar from a sliver
of shrapnel spun from a cloud of cluster bombs
exploding over Can Tho, Tet Offensive, 1968.

"Wounded and missing" they telegrammed his kin,
but he knew where he was all the time. Sort of.

HEAD: concussion, age 30; wife cracked a skillet on his head.
Even *he* thought he deserved it. (No further comment.)
But the girl's name was not "Betty." *Elizabeth.*

SPINE: his X-rays at middle age show an ominous shadow,
but it's just arthritis from jammed-up ribs. Thrown off
a horse in Las Trucas, N.M. Too drunk to hang on.

LEFT SHOULDER, three rips on the rotator cuff.
From bucking a chain saw for two straight weeks,
cutting oaks and banyans off their Miami house.

In the hurricane debris, in the blistering heat,
broken snakes and iguanas, dead tree frogs,
woodpecker hatchlings. Sawteeth screaming.

HEAD: concussion, age 50, New Mexico. Another horse.
(What did they smell? Booze? Bravura?)

LEFT HAND, broken little finger, reattached with a pin.
The "boxer's break," the surgeon said. Claimed
a board fell back and split his fingers.

FRONT TOOTH: chipped. Chomped down in so much rage
as he swung at the guy, he broke his own tooth.
(Still a bit slow regarding consequences.)

FACE: no visible scarring.
The poet smiles as he walks on stage.

Miami Suite

A Note to Hayden Carruth from Miami

Here, where orchids scent our evenings
and the sapodilla drops its spotted fruit,
gray, gritty, sweet, I raise a glass
of the "poet's cheap, sufficient chardonnay"
and salute your freezing northern nights,

your days in the muddy slop of springtime
when trillium unfurls its delicate tongue,
where skunk cabbage unwinds in the icy bog,
and bleeding heart trembles in Isabel's garden.
We've never met and probably never will

except in the imagined land of green things
beyond your daughter's death, beyond folly,
beyond fame, beyond indignation and pain,
toasting the first life in small things
fresh from the earth with their tentative yes.

Butter People

In Spain, just after the First World War,
some goatherds in the mountains near Málaga
caught two of them wandering a barranca,
those steep ravines creasing dry slopes
glinting in sunny haze, dropping south
to the sea, to the distant etch of Africa.
Mantequeros: "butter people."

                     Empty-eyed,
blubbery, pale creatures babbling nonsense,
child-stealers, *child-killers* who look human
until you see them close. But these two,
heads yanked back, squealing at razors pressed
to their throats were, as it turned out, just lost Englishmen
looking for Señor Brennan who lived outside of town.

Tibetan monks, sealed up in caves for months
might sometimes make a figure out of butter,
chants, and visualizations, a companion so real
that others could see it riding with them
saddled on a pony when they left the anchorite cliffs.
These man-made demons would always decompose,
turning on their masters until dispatched by spells.
Myamin: "not men," hungry to ravage and destroy.

Exotic legends perhaps, although today
my daughter brought home from school
a list of "local registered sexual predators,"
thirty-nine men, with xeroxed mug shots

and addresses: Gilberto Dominquay, 65 years old,
6' tall. Yves Champagne, Eddie Scott Garle,
Rafael Garrido whose picture, like others,
is "not yet received," his address "unknown."

In the fuzzy photos, they look human enough.
Like men here who mow yards, maybe mend a screen.

Some Notes on Miami

SNAILS

slide across the air-conditioned glass
as morning sun plunges through our windows.
Poor disoriented mollusks, gliding nowhere but easily
in glissando waltz through beads of condensation
stretching out their knobby eyes for the aubade's edge,
for stone's shade below *las flores*, in Florida.

PARROTS

With half the trees derived from Africa or Asia
perhaps even parrots will replace the native birds,
or so this pair of cracker doves, perched on a wire,
seem to nod to each other,
as parrots thrash the mango leaves
shrieking tree to tree.

Parrot, lorikeet, roller, toucan — all
loosed from cages and free in Miami —
assault the air with raucous squawks,
calling up flocks for their new world order.

ALLIGATOR

How could any creature that might spend eternity
as pocketbook or pair of shoes, or simply
trapped in a sinkhole, take the risk?
Rising off the mucky bottom, roiling the river,
plated brow specked with duckweed, jaws
lunging up, clamping on the child's head,

dragging him under, as his father
bashed the water with an oar, how?
After dissection, the vet said
it looked hungry. El Lagarto: the lizard.

HURRICANE

Naked, floating facedown in the TV room
now filled with seawater seeping from glass doors
he had duct-taped against the hurricane,
the room a dark aquarium, his white body, bobbing
— he must have been asleep on the couch, exhausted
after a day of battening down the house
when baysurge beached in a swarm of seaspouts
churning up the mangrove swamp, the great wave colliding,
breaching doors, collapsing walls, wallowing, then
tumbling back out as winds shrieked off treetops,
sea slosh sucking up drowned frogs, broken snakes,
skinned pelicans, dragging leaf muck, sparkles of
shattered glass, lawn chairs, rolling a dead manatee,
slopping back through tangles of trees, impaled boats,
to the seesaw bay sizzling with rain, leaving him
rocking in a kelp of curtains, arms outstretched
toward something in the green cloudy water.

THE CUBAN RAFTER

At the dock behind his house in Islamorada
he cranks the windlass and lifts his boat from the bay.
Below, lobsters tickle antennae at murky pilings
while the ibis paces the jetty, anxious
for any prawns brought back in the bucket,
for wrasse and yellowtails languid in their pails.

But now, barebacked, bending to the weight on the winch,
ignoring the frantic bird, the freckled man pulls up his boat,
the scar across his shoulder just a purply burl
in the rose light of evening.
                              Boat secured,
he studies the reef where his raft had drifted
into... *the snorkeling school from the Cheeca Lodge,*
the divers' eyes big, big behind their masks,
all waving to come see him, burnt-faced, silent,
lying on a wooden raft, alone upon the waves...
"Hola, primo," he says to the manatee rising by the dock
like a luminous submarine, "Hola," he says,
and reaches in a hamper for heads of lettuce saved
for this prop-scarred blimp that begs its dinners
from wealthy docks along the Key,
from him, now the "guayabera shirt king of Miami"
whose raft was waterless on the sixth day out
who landed here without his wife
her last words whimpered through blistered lips
before she rolled off under a Bahamian swell,
whose first job was janitor at the Biltmore
whose melanoma almost ate his socket out
who made six million dollars in eighteen years
who now has a family and house in Hialeah
and who comes here alone when he can on weekends
to chase kingfish and snook, to listen to wavewash,
to toss baits to the loony bird haunting his dock
to drop a hose to the manatee thirsty for freshwater,
whom he calls his "cousin" and tells to drink.

Gwanes they have, which is a little harmlesse beast,
like a Crokadell or Aligator, very fat and good meat.

CAPTAIN JOHN SMITH, 1630

Iwana [Carib], Iuanna, Wana, Gwane, Iguana.
There's the common green iguana from Colombia
that eats hibiscus and bananas
and its cousin, *iguana delicatissima*,
which indicates the problem for this harmless beast:
gallina del palo, they call it in Spanish
in *las Americas* and throughout the Caribbean:
"chicken of the tree."
                    Mr. Dieu-Donné Telforêt,
Monsieur "Given-by-God from the Distant Forest,"
my Haitian cabbie who takes me into town,
keeps his iguana in a halter on the passenger seat,
whether as dinner or *amie* I can't say.

SATURDAY NIGHT

At Bayside, a crowd enjoys an outdoor concert
as lasers shoot green streaks across the sky.
On South Beach the kids parade in silly clothing.
In Hialeah, there's a meeting of Alpha 66. Somewhere
the *santeríos* are cutting throats of chickens.
Everywhere the rich are showing off their wealth.
While at a darkened Wal-Mart where the Everglades begin,
inside the Garden Shop, at wilderness's edge,
green-glow *cucuyo* fireflies light rows of oleander
and a swamp rattler curls inside a potted palm.

Rising off the droughts of Africa, the dry pans
of the Atlas Mountains, the Sahara, the El Djouf,
swirling up from parched fields, the rich dust
sails on stratospheric winds across the Atlantic,
sifts down onto the Amazon, rains upon the Everglades,
falling here this Sunday morning, in Miami
where we brush it from our cars, perplexed.

Eddie

Hadn't seen Eddie for some time,
wheeling his chair through traffic,
skinny legs in shorts, T-shirted,
down at the corner off Dixie Highway,
lifting his Coke cup to the drivers
backed up, bumper to bumper, at the light.
Sometimes he slept on the concrete bench
up from Joe's News. Sometimes police
would haul him in and he said he didn't mind
because he got three squares and sometimes
a doctor would look at his legs, paralyzed,
he said, since the cop in New York shot him
when he tried to steal a car. Sad story,
of the kind we've learned to live with.

One rainy day he looked so bad, legs
ballooned, ankles to calves, clothes soaked,
I shoved a $20 in his cup. But, like I said,
I hadn't seen him around so yesterday
I stopped and asked this other panhandler,
Where's Eddie? "Dead," he said. Slammed
by a truck running the light, crushed
into his wheelchair. Dead, months ago.

My wife says he's better off dead,
but I don't know. Behind his smudged glasses
his eyes were clever. He had a goofy smile
but his patter was sharp. His legs were a mess
and he had to be lonely. But spending days

in the bright fanfare of traffic and
those nights on his bench, with the moon
huge in the palm trees, the highway quiet,
some good dreams must have come to him.

Dinner in Miami

APPETIZER

> We may live without friends; we may live without books;
> But civilized man cannot live without cooks.
>
> EDWARD ROBERT BULWER, EARL OF LYTTON,
> *Lucile*

ENTRÉE

The worn-out man and his red-eyed wife
had driven up from the Keys at the end of an awful day
spent wrangling with a son, bankrupt once again.
It might have perked them up, had they known
their chef once cooked for Princess Grace.
Maybe not. "You are what you eat. Eat what you are,"
the man declared, downing his stiff drink to order
the bourbon-soaked rib eye with orange chimichurri.
His wife sighed and could not decide
between the Key West yellowtail
and the cassoulet with confit of duck.

Their lives improved with the appetizers,
the truffled sauce, the capers in conch piccata,
with the ample portions on oversized plates,
the good wine, the sweet light in the clear glass lamp,
all reminding them of better times, of Paris,
of restaurants on the boulevard St. Germaine,
the Luxembourg Gardens, the lights on the Seine,
the honeymoon that continued on to Málaga.
"Remember that gypsy singer at El Figon?" he asked,
both of them now looking at the list of desserts,

"The one who called himself El Chocolaté?"
She smiled a wide Princess Grace of a smile.
And he, although not given to public displays,
took her hand and kissed it.

DESSERT

Chocolate Crunch Bar
with vanilla anglaise, strawberry sauce
and chocolate cigarette

Chocolate [*chocolatl*, from the Mayan *xocoatl*].
The Aztec royal drink chilled with mountain snow
frothed and spiced with honeyed cloves.
Montezuma drank it before going to his wives.
Cortés shipped it home in 1528. Now the couple
shares a plate, while sipping at their sherry,
remembering the song El Chocolaté sang:

> *When will the day come,*
> *that blissful morning when*
> *chocolate will be brought to us*
> *side by side in bed?*

Both of them now grateful, near the end of day,
for dinners that offer ease like poetry or song.

Big Boy

He wasn't so charming at first:
      huge-headed, black feral cat
hissing on our doorstep,
      marking territory, pissing up the patio
so that when you slid open the glass doors
      expecting jasmine or gardenia
you got cat stench
      and yowling in the bushes
as he raked and thrashed his mangy rivals.

Even our dogs ran off when he rushed them.
      But my daughter fed and coaxed him in
until at last he let her pick him up
      cradled like some fanged, wild-eyed baby.

And now, he's all hers, dozing in the ferns
      until she comes home from school,
then padding out to greet her on the driveway
      eager for her scratch
      on his scarred-up head,
domesticated, like me, by her sweet voice.

After Hurricane Andrew

Near dawn our old live oak sagged over
crashed on the toolshed
rocketing off rakes paint cans flowerpots.

Rain slashed the shutters all night until
it quit and day arrived in queer light,
silence, and ozoned air. Then voices calling

as neighbors crept out to see the snapped trees,
leaf mash and lawn chairs driven in heaps
with roof bits, siding, sodden birds, dead snakes.

For days, Army cranes clanked by our houses
in sickening August heat as bulldozers
scraped the rotting tonnage from the streets.

Then our friend Elling drove over from Sarasota
in his old VW van packed with candles, with
dog food, cat food, flashlights and batteries,

jugs of water, a frozen cake, crackers and caviar,
a case of Tsingtao beer, some chainsaw blades,
and tropical trees to plant the place again.

Five years later, the ylang-ylang rises
thirty feet, unfurling long yellow blossoms
to fill our evenings with essence of Chanel.

And so it goes with the *Pritchardia* palms,
the gumbo limbo, Cuban guanabana,
papaya, bananas, and bamboo. Now the house

is shaded, overhung with bougainvillea,
trellised in passion flower, scented by gardenia,
by Burmese orchids that drink our humid air,

each offering its reply to wreckage.

Remembering Miami

A breeze shoves in off Key Biscayne,
stirring the heavy evening air,
trembling gardenia and ylang-ylang

perfuming the patio where he sits
like a genie in an old perfume bottle
reading the newspaper, drink in hand.

His prize koi circles the pond
like a slow thought. The fountain
drips its meditative trickle. Inside,

his daughter is baking brownies
and his wife is taking a snooze.
Damp air blots the *Herald*'s news

of the D.A. led off in handcuffs
for biting a naked table dancer, while,
elsewhere, *a dead fish and six coins*

were left on the Mayor's doorstep,
and, in Homestead, *a 10-foot anaconda*
was hauled out from under a house.

Above his chair, a flock of parrots
are squawking in the sea grape tree,
worried by dozens of wheeling vultures.

A police siren screams off down the street.
He finishes his drink and goes inside.
The damn place never made any sense.

Anna Akhmatova Spends the Night on Miami Beach

Well, her book, anyway. The Kunitz volume
left lying on a bench, the pages
a bit puffy by morning, flushed with dew,
riffled by sea breeze, scratchy with sand
— the paperback with the 1930s photo
showing her in spangled caftan, its back cover
calling her "star of the St. Petersburg circle
of Pasternak, Mandelstam, and Blok,
surviving the Revolution and two World Wars."

So she'd been through worse…
the months outside Lefortovo prison
waiting for a son exiled to Siberia, watching
women stagger and reel with news of executions,
one mother asking, "Can you write about this?"
Akhmatova thought, then answered, "Yes."

If music lured her off the sandy bench
to the clubs where men were kissing
that wouldn't have bothered her much,
nor the vamps shashaying in leather.
Decadence amid art deco fit nicely
with her black dress, chopped hair, Chanel cap.
What killed her was the talk, the empty eyes,
which made her long for the one person in ten thousand
who could say her name in Russian,
who could take her home, giving her a place
next to Auden and Apollinaire,

to whom she could describe her night's excursion
amid the loud hilarities, the trivial hungers
at the end of the American century.

A Little Story

There must have been thirty of us, writers from maybe twenty nations, in that smoky bar of the villa that belonged to the Union of Bulgarian Writers, though perhaps only God and a few Party officials (and maybe somebody with a yellowed deed living in a déclassé arrondissement of Paris) might have really known who the State took it from or if it was actually built from Marxist labor, that is, from the farmers who produced the corn and peas and attar of roses for European markets, or the metal castings for light industries, or the cargo ships. Anyway, it was in Varna, the port where Dracula set sail for England.

Kolyo Sevov—a giant with a great straggly beard who had been a sea captain before turning to poetry—had brought in the chief of police who was sweating in his rumpled blue uniform despite the sea air pouring through the door that a barmaid had propped open to let out smoke. The Chief had downed a Scotch-and-soda, and now was telling a story—which stirred the translators to drunken mumbles—of his bad, but (he emphasized) *typical* summer day in that some French tourists...

—"they do this every goddamn year!" he shouted, mopping his bald head and adding, in the general direction of French mumbling, "No offense.

"...anyway," he continued, "every summer they go up on the hotel roof and take the Bulgarian flag down from the flagpole and then run up the French tricolor and every summer I have to send some young cop up to take it down and, you know, someday someone is going to fall and get hurt.

"But worse, yesterday we had to take out another dead Finn." He finished his second whisky and looked around the quieted room, explaining, "They fly in here whacked on airplane vodka, check in, never leave their hotel bar or, sometimes, even their rooms, but just drink themselves to death on our cheap booze. We carry out at least two every summer. They look as white as the bathtub. You know what a legal mess it is to ship a foreign corpse?"

Just then Ulla's little girl ran in—blond hair whisking her tanned bony shoulders—and glancing about the room of boozers shouting at one another over the thump of the sound system, came over to me calling in Swedish and pulling at my hand, pulling me up out of my chair toward the open door as Rockwell sang "sometimes I feel like somebody's watching me," and I staggered up and looked at Ulla, who looked perplexed, and then heard someone say, as the child kept pulling me to the door, "Hey, Johnny. You have a girlfriend," and then, once I was outside, all the laughter, disco, and bar babble were… shushed by the huge starry sky and the crash of waves on this edge of Europe where a Turkish moon hung like a scimitar over the sea.

"Anna, where are we going," I asked, as she yanked me down the steep slope and nodded yes, her little hand in mine as we passed under terraced cherry trees just bearing fruit and I followed along down a stairway of limestone blocks as the sea below heaved and gasped in darkness and the moonlit surf rattled stones and tumbling shells.

"Anna?"

Now she was ahead and waving me on across a grassy hillside damp with salt mists blowing inland and I had to stoop to follow her into bushes where she finally stopped and knelt before a clump of grass, a little clutch of weeds, where fireflies pulsed in a lantern of soft lights flickering in her eyes as she turned to see if I saw, to see if I understood.

Well, that was decades ago. Little stranger. Bright firefly.

Varna Snow

for Roland Flint

> Often, gates shut, safe inside the walls,
> we gather arrows fallen in the streets.
>
> OVID, *Tristia* V.x:21–22

A breeze riffles in off the beach
stirring poplar catkins, wooly stuff
drifting the town in flurries, searching

the air like syllables of poetry while
we perch on the stones of this Roman bath
listening to poetry, the delicate thing which lasts.

Here at the edge of empires, boys, silly with love,
chatted idly by the pools. Merchants,
trading amphoras of oil and Lydian dye,

cursed thin profits, cruel seas, lost ships.
Now seagulls flap and squawk on broken walls
scurfed with weeds and the royal poppy.

Greek and Roman, Getae, Thracian, Bulgar,
Slavs, Avars, Goths, Celts, Tatars, Huns,
Arabs, Turks, Russians, and, now, the U.S. Navy.

Not far from here, one frigid winter in Tomis,
an aging Ovid, exiled by Augustus,
donned a helmet to defend the ramparts

as Thracian horsemen circled the frozen marsh,
their long hair tinkling with chinks of ice,
shooting poisoned arrows into the walled city

killing the boy who attended the old poet,
the boy he paid to massage his skin, there
in "the last place," among barbarians

two thousand years ago. But, now, acacias
fragrance our evening as poplar fluff drifts
through imperial rubble. Only poetry lasts.

Van Gogh

translated from the Bulgarian with the author,
Lyubomir Nikolov

Well, he lived among us and hated winters.
He moved to Arles where summer and blue jays
obliged him to cut off his ear.
Oh, they all said it was a whore
but Rachel was innocent. When cypresses
went for a walk in the prison yard
he went along and sketched them.
His suns surpassed God's.
He spelled out the Gospel for miners
and their potatoes stuck in his throat.
Yes, he was a priest in sackcloth, who hoped
that one day humans would learn to walk.
He willed mankind his shoes.

Dr. Alice Magheru's Room

What a mess. The walls cluttered with paintings,
sketches, portraits. Photos: your father-in-law,
Prince Ghica of Samos, and his wife Alexandrina
who played piano with Liszt and Clara Schumann.
Carmen Silva, at her desk, pen in hand. A poem
she wrote for you in feathery blue ink.
The royal family posed beside a car.
A note from Queen Helene that calls you "dear."
Enescu and his nephew walking to a train.
A lithograph of General Magheru, muttonchopped

hero of the Turkish war, staring resolutely
across the Black Sea, hand on his sword hilt.
And books. Everywhere. Eight thousand books
piled on the floor, crammed into shelves, sliding
off desktops. Your husband's books of poetry,
his "antipoems" that had more vogue in France
and — leatherbound, titled in thin gold Roman type —
the medical texts you published together.
Bacteriologist, serologist, immunologist,
you made pills as the British bombed Bucharest.

Each night you nap like a cat and read
while others sleep, stretching your eighty-seven
years into twice their human span. Last night
you spoke with your husband, dead for twenty years.
Today, you banter with a poet from America
whose taxi, when he leaves, rattles tram tracks
and cobblestones, halts at a light,

then nudges through crowds on Magheru Boulevard.
Earthquakes and armies have rolled down this street.
You've seen them come and go.

Like sound, the human spirit never dies
but fades, falters, filters off through space,
or is trapped in the laths of marble hearts.
In the quarries of the Parthenon
the shouts of masons murmur still,
caught in crystals like the quartz radio
I played with as a child. So it is, Alice,
with a soul sent out to others, signaling
from this room, this cell of powerful repose,
over the long years: the conscious mind.

Driving Back East with My Dad

I still see him through the Instamatic, standing
before the Great Sand Dunes of the southern Rockies,
a slow wind pulling streams of sand across his knees
as the dunes loomed behind him and he squinted
at the camera, baseball cap over his long white hair.
Seventy-five, and about to ride 2,000 miles in my old pickup.

In his Romanian village, he is still remembered
for making, age 12, a die for counterfeiting coins.
At 14, not that long after the Wright brothers
and Kitty Hawk, he flew his model plane
over the cornfields of his Schwabe neighbors.
In his village of geese and corn bins, he studied calculus.
Once, he saved a boy nearly pecked to death by geese.
By 18, he was a roundhouse foreman in the Carpathians.
At 19, swimming the Danube to an island where Turks
sold their heavenly tobacco, he almost drowned
until a Tatar girl jumped in to haul him out.

At 21, he came here with scarcely a word of English,
joined the U.S. Army as a Cavalry officer, but was obliged
to resign his commission for clobbering his superior
with a weighted riding crop. In World War II,
working at the Philadelphia Naval Yard, he invented
the C130 "Flying Boxcar." (I still have his blueprints.)
After the war, in Scranton, lunching with his staff of engineers,
he made them march out of the Purple Cow restaurant
when the maître d' wouldn't serve his black draftsman.
One of his inventions — a step ladder/ironing board/high chair

—got us on a '50s TV show called *The Big Idea*,
where I climbed up in the high chair in my little suit.
He went bankrupt; had a wicked temper,
once mortifying my mother by tossing her bowl of soup
into a rude waiter's face, and chasing him into the kitchen.
At 16, after one of his punch-ups, I ran away from home.

Can't say we said much on our drive,
a mere detour on his long crooked path.
As the miles rolled past, we only stopped
for diner food, gas, and motels where we'd sip
his Jack Daniel's and watch TV from our beds.
Five days of driving, with a biblical start:
black skies slamming down thunder,
rips of lightning, and even a tornado
that churned up a wheat field near Limon
as we rattled along into Kansas,
hail whacking my truck, thumping off
the cab and hood and clattering the backbed with ice.
He just turned off his hearing aid, and Sphinx-like
seemed pleased with his ride through the high plains.

How I wish for a lyric ending to this prose tale:
a moment when the travelers, going in the direction
they faced, found they had already arrived. Still,
it was good, being alive together, taking in the road,
mindful of where we had come, and moving on.

The Goodbyes

What have I become?
My sweetest friend
Everyone I know
Goes away in the end.

JOHNNY CASH, SINGING TRENT REZNOR'S "HURT"

Our last farewells may come as a surprise.
Whether we made our preparations, or never bothered.

For some, it's *au revoir*; for others, just goodbye.
Or "oops" or even "no!" but, still, a final moment of *me*.

Losing others goes on longer, both the dead and alive
Who we will never see again but in dream or memory.

Whisper their names into your pillow at bedtime.
Say them all you want, you are calling after ghosts:

Dead parents, good or bad, dwelling in terminal silence.
Ex's living in Ohio with someone you've never met.

Past lovers, old friends, homes you had, last replies.
Lips you kissed, would kiss again. Children grown and gone.

This is our harder trial; these, our bleakest times:
Not our own going, but the going of others.

The Great Fugue

for Ruth and Don Beatty, for Ella and Tom Rhoads,
and for Lorraine and Paul Sensenig

Amp up, needle dropping down
onto the sheen of spinning vinyl,
releasing a screech of cries
a surge of voices
as mute tongues locked in silence
break free
break through
in tumults of twined calls
filling my room
with this old recording
given me some forty years ago
when I was 16 and a runaway.

Taken in by teachers, I became their project
as big snows banked the lanes of Bucks County farms,
their red snowfences almost buried now
under the cement sprawl of the Eastern Seaboard.

That senior year, I lived with the art teacher
and her husband who put me to work splitting firewood
and shoveling snow. "Cord wood warms you twice,"
he liked to say, as he taught me how to swing a sledge
that long winter when I drove with his wife to school,
the kids in the parking lot staring at me weirdly.

Out on the snowstorm Delaware, ice sheets
bob the currents, sliding up onto pilings

of the footbridge near the Black Bass Inn
with its snow-swept colonial fieldstone.
Buffets of sleet tumble into the whipped, leaden water
where a line of Canada geese paddle upstream,
beaks dipped into the gale, fighting the river.

The cornfields on the distant Jersey banks
rage with snow devils of ripped-up snowcrust,
swirling bits of blasted stalk and broken sheaves
all spinning in the storm

over this river where America began
one snowy night, one unlikely eve, just downriver
when the tall courtly general with bad teeth
risked all, including his head, in a doubtful raid
across the fierce dark water
to rout the Hessians drunk in Christmas slumber.

After spring's blush of crocus and forsythia,
other teachers hired me to rake their yards,
trim hedges, lay cinder block, and so I had a little cash,
and when the redbuds and dogwoods flowered
and the shadbushes were shaking white blossoms,
and the shad were running at Washington Crossing,
my mentors' discreet collusions kept me from running off
to the territories, to an East Coast dream of California.

Just a kid perched in a mulberry tree,
I watched the car enter the abandoned farm
now flagged and dotted with surveyor stakes,
the white Mercedes bouncing through a swale
of black-eyed Susans and Queen Ann's lace,
daisy heads slapping the wheelwells until the car

stopped and two men in three-piece suits
got out to open a map and point to a fieldstone hedgerow
overgrown with sumac and walnut and blackberry tangles
at the edge of a wood near the River Road
by the old canal, by its towpath, where a bulldozer
idled by a long gash of Delaware bottomland.

My civics teacher pushed me hard in class.
At school, she would not let me sulk; at her home
she paid me to alphabetize her books and records,
all of it a ruse to get them in my hands. "This one?"
I asked her wizened husband, Tom. "Play it?"
I held up the *Grosse Fugue*, Budapest String Quartet.
"Oh, no," he said. "I only play that once a year.
Maybe," he thought a moment, "we'll hear it at Easter."

He had an original, signed, cerulean blue edition
of *Ulysses* that he got in Paris at Shakespeare and Company
that evening when a jittery Joyce debuted his book.
I wanted to read Joyce. "Oh, John," Tom said, "first
you have to read Homer." And when I read Homer,
he suggested Tennyson, and when I read Tennyson,
he thought I might like Nikos Kazantzakis,
and then he gave me his Modern Library *Ulysses*.
Tom was so old, he had agitated against the First World War,
so alcoholic as a young man in Texas,
they put him on a train and sent him home to die.
In class, his wife needled me but won my heart
with a newspaper photo that nearly got her fired:
standing in a manure wagon dumped by a local farmer
in front of the town hall in rural Point Pleasant,
behind her the Delaware flowing past sycamores
as she railed to a small crowd against "The Pump"

built by Philadelphia Electric to flush 90 million gallons
(per day) to cool its nuclear reactor at Limerick.

> *When the English longboat left its ship,*
> *it approached a shoreline populated by Lenni-Lenape,*
> *quite startling savages, near naked, with bows and spears.*
> *Lord Delaware, who led the party in service of George III,*
> *was closely guarded by twelve marines.*
> *But neither side raised gun nor bow and, as the ledger says,*
> *the Indians, who seemed amicable, quickly declared*
> *"Ne Na Nah De La Wah" ("We are men of men")*
> *causing an aide-de-camp, on hearing "De La Wah," to comment,*
> *"I say, My Lord,*
> *your fame precedes you even onto these heathen parts."*

Now that lovely farmland is mostly turned to malls.
The woods behind my boyhood house — where I found
arrowheads, box turtles, musket balls, and, once,
a bayonet from the Revolutionary War — are all gone.
My wise elders are long dead. Today is Easter.
I imagine spring rains in whatever fields the developers have left.
By the swift currents of Upper Black Eddy, the river's banks
will already have unfurled in mayapple and fern.
Easter, and I am playing the *Grosse Fugue*, hearing
the faded voices of those good people
who did not want to see me falter, but took me in,
schooling me in an intertwining of spirits
that like music can fill a room, that is a great fugue
weaving through us and joining generations
in charged, exquisite music that we long to hear.

About the Author

John Balaban is the author of twelve books of poetry and prose, including four volumes that together have won the Academy of American Poets' Lamont Prize, a National Poetry Series selection, and two nominations for the National Book Award. His *Locusts at the Edge of Summer: New and Selected Poems* won the 1998 William Carlos Willams Award from the Poetry Society of America. In 2003, he was awarded a John Simon Guggenheim fellowship.

In addition to writing poetry, fiction, and nonfiction, he is a translator of Vietnamese poetry and a past president of the American Literary Translators Association.

Balaban is poet in residence and professor of English at North Carolina State University in Raleigh.

The Chinese character for poetry is made up of two parts: "word" and "temple." It also serves as pressmark for Copper Canyon Press. Founded in 1972, Copper Canyon Press remains dedicated to publishing poetry exclusively, from Nobel laureates to new and emerging authors. The Press thrives with the generous patronage of readers, writers, booksellers, librarians, teachers, students, and funders — everyone who shares the conviction that poetry invigorates the language and sharpens our appreciation of the world.

Major funding has been provided by:

Anonymous (2)

The Paul G. Allen Family Foundation

Lannan Foundation

National Endowment for the Arts

Washington State Arts Commission

THE **PAUL G. ALLEN** **FAMILY** *foundation*

Lannan

NATIONAL
ENDOWMENT
FOR THE ARTS

WASHINGTON
STATE ARTS
COMMISSION

For information and catalogs:

COPPER CANYON PRESS

Post Office Box 271
Port Townsend, Washington 98368
360-385-4925
www.coppercanyonpress.org

Path, Crooked Path is set in MVB Verdigris, a text face by Mark van Bronkhorst and inspired by the sixteenth-century typefaces of Robert Granjon (roman) and Pierre Haultin (italic). The display titles are set in Interstate, designed by Tobias Frere-Jones based on the signs of the United States Federal Highway Administration. Book design by Valerie Brewster, Scribe Typography. Printed on archival-quality Glatfelter Author's Text at McNaughton & Gunn, Inc.